PUZZLE PENGUINS

A MAZE ADVENTURE

Written, illustrated, & designed by

PATRICK MERRELL

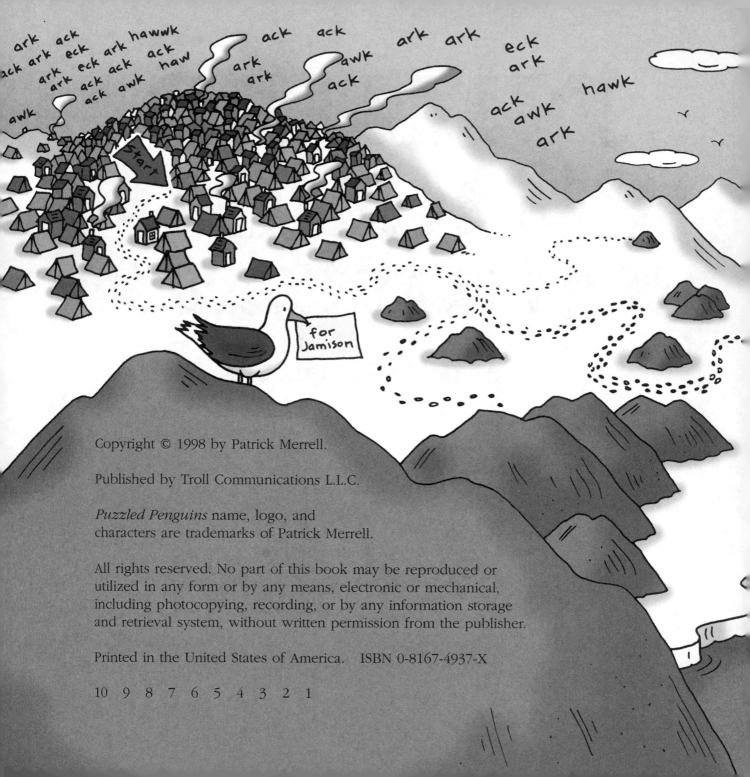

Herbert and Martha Penguin's neighborhood had become crowded and noisy.
They decided a nice spot near the water would be better.
"Ahhh, this is the life," Herbert said with a sigh.
"Lovely," Martha agreed.

Can you follow the path they took to get to their new home?

The next morning, Herbert poked his head out of their tent.
"Where did all these icebergs come from?" he wondered.
"We've drifted out to sea!" Martha cried.
They were far from home—and headed right for a big rock!
"Start paddling!" Martha called.

Can you find a route that will get them safely through these icebergs?

"Now what do we do?" Martha asked.
"I've got an idea," Herbert said. "My trusty compass!"
But as Herbert pulled the compass out of his hat, it
slipped and dropped into the ocean.
"Ack!!" he squealed. "My compass!"
They both dived in after it.

Can you find a path through this bed of tangled
seaweed to Herbert's compass?

Unfortunately, Herbert's compass was now filled with water. It was useless.

"BLAAAAAAGGG!" a loud horn blasted.

"It's a ship!" Martha said.

"Let's go check it out!" Herbert suggested.

Can you get Herbert and Martha through these rocks to the ship?

By the time they got to the ship, their ice raft had begun to melt.

Martha rolled up the tent to make more room. The ice was still barely big enough for the two of them.

"Grab one of those ropes!" Martha cried.

"Which one?" Herbert asked.

One of these ropes will lower the rope ladder down to Herbert and Martha. Can you figure out which one it is?

It had been a long morning, and neither of them had had anything to eat.

"I'm hungry," Herbert grumbled.

"Me too," Martha agreed. "Where do you suppose they keep the food around here?"

Using this wall map, can you find a way for Herbert and Martha to get to the kitchen?

Inside the kitchen, two cooks were busy making lunch.
"Yuk," Herbert whispered. "They're making pizza!"
"But look," Martha replied. "It's anchovy pizza!"
Anchovies were their favorite fish.
"Yum," they both said, licking their beaks.

Can you help Herbert and Martha sneak past the cooks
and get to the cans of yummy anchovies?

After their snack, the penguins waddled back out on deck. Herbert heard a familiar sound in the distance, "Ark! Ark!"

"I'd know that sound anywhere," Herbert gasped. "Penguins!" Martha picked up a telescope. "They're on that island," she said, "but how do we get there?"

"Quick!" Herbert squawked. "Grab a balloon."

Can you follow the paths that Herbert and Martha took?

Start

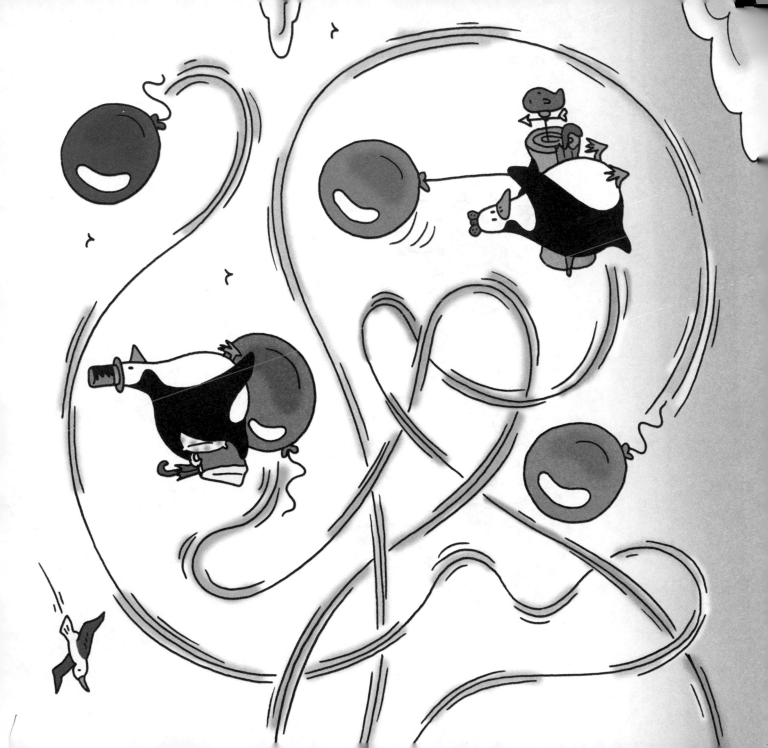

A gentle breeze blew Herbert and Martha right over the island.
They pulled out their umbrellas and then let go of the balloons.

Can you get *both* of them through these clouds and down to the island?

"Plop!"
Herbert landed on a sandbar just off the island.
"Plunk!"
Martha landed in a rowboat.

Can you find a way for Martha to row to Herbert and *then* to the island?

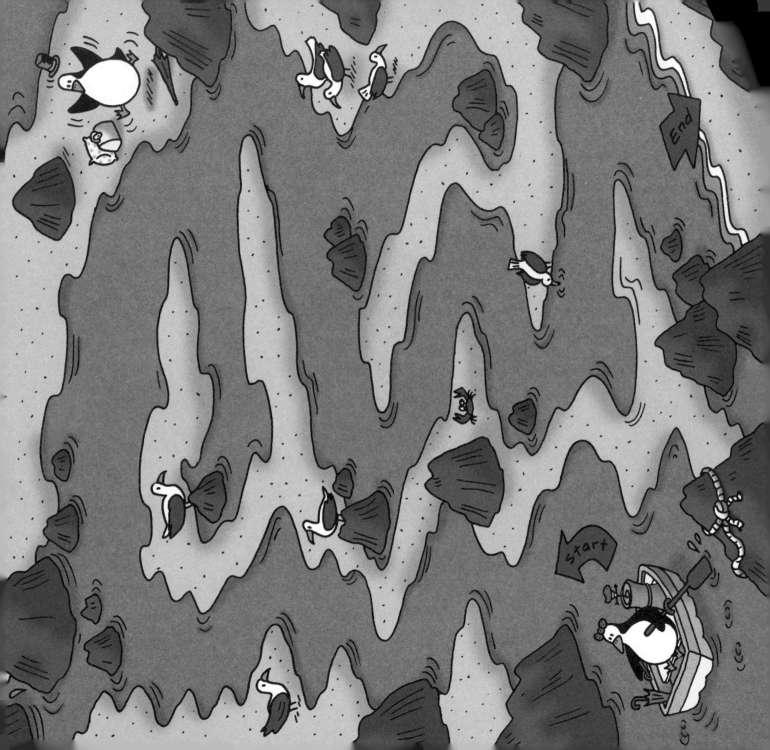

There was a large cliff at the edge of the island. "Welcome to Rockhopper Island," said a sign at the bottom of the cliff.

"Come on up," a penguin called from the top of the cliff.

Can you find a path up to the top?

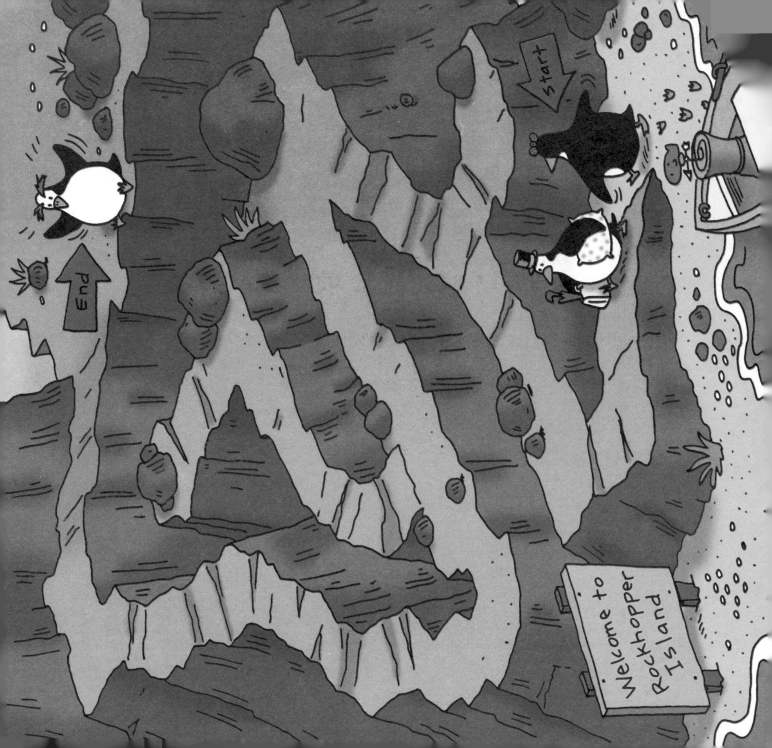

At the top of the cliff stood a large colony of rockhopper penguins.

"What's with their crazy hairdos?" Herbert whispered.

"Shhh," Martha said. "That's just the way their feathers grow."

One of the rockhoppers had an idea about how Herbert and Martha could find their home.

"Molly the albatross," he said. "She'll know where your home is."

"But how do we find *her*?" Herbert puzzled.

"Right across this field," the rockhopper said. "You can't miss her."

Can you find the way through this crowd of rockhopper penguins to Molly the albatross?

Molly was a wise old bird who knew just about everything.

Best of all, she knew how to get to Herbert and Martha's island.

"You've come a long way," she said, "but you should be able to make it home by the end of the day."

She drew a map to show them.

Can you find the way home on this map?

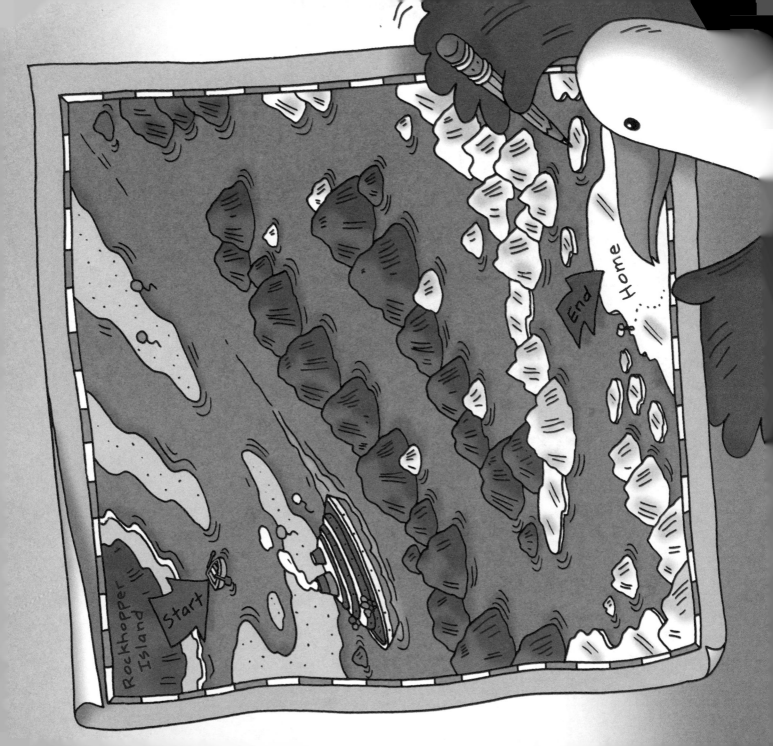

Herbert and Martha scurried back to the rowboat.
They rowed and rowed and rowed.
Finally, they spotted their home.
"Ark, ark!" Herbert cried.
"Let's go!" Martha clucked.
They grabbed their things and dived into the water.

Can you find the way through the water to their island?

When they reached the island, they waddled to their old home as quickly as they could.

"Ahhh, this is the life," Herbert said with a sigh.

"Lovely," Martha agreed.

And they couldn't have been happier.

Start

Can you find the path they took to get to their old home? Congratulations!

PENGUIN FACTS

Penguins are excellent swimmers. They can swim through the water as fast as a blue jay can fly through the sky.

- Penguins live only in the southern part of the world—almost all of them near the South Pole.

- A single colony of penguins can have more than a million birds. The noise—and smell—can be overpowering.

- *Rockhopper* penguins hop like kangaroos up and down steep cliffs.

- Male *emperor* penguins warm eggs on their feet during the winter. They won't move from the eggs for two months—even to eat!

- Thick feathers and a layer of fat keep penguins warm.